ALL AROUND THE WORLD
GERMANY

by Jessica Dean

Ideas for Parents and Teachers

Pogo Books let children practice reading informational text while introducing them to nonfiction features such as headings, labels, sidebars, maps, and diagrams, as well as a table of contents, glossary, and index.

Carefully leveled text with a strong photo match offers early fluent readers the support they need to succeed.

Before Reading

- "Walk" through the book and point out the various nonfiction features. Ask the student what purpose each feature serves.
- Look at the glossary together. Read and discuss the words.

Read the Book

- Have the child read the book independently.
- Invite him or her to list questions that arise from reading.

After Reading

- Discuss the child's questions. Talk about how he or she might find answers to those questions.
- Prompt the child to think more. Ask: Germany still has castles throughout the country that kings and queens once lived in. Can you think of any large buildings for leaders that are found throughout your country?

Pogo Books are published by Jump!
5357 Penn Avenue South
Minneapolis, MN 55419
www.jumplibrary.com

Library of Congress Cataloging-in-Publication Data

Names: Dean, Jessica, 1963- author.
Title: Germany : all around the world / by Jessica Dean.
Description: Minneapolis, MN : Pogo Books, Jump!, Inc., 2019.
Series: All around the world | Includes index.
Identifiers: LCCN 2018018392 (print)
LCCN 2018020037 (ebook)
ISBN 9781641281607 (ebook)
ISBN 9781641281584 (hardcover : alk. paper)
ISBN 9781641281591 (pbk.)
Subjects: LCSH: Germany—Juvenile literature.
Classification: LCC DD17 (ebook)
LCC DD17 .D3554 2019 (print) | DDC 943—dc23
LC record available at https://lccn.loc.gov/2018018392

Editor: Kristine Spanier
Designer: Molly Ballanger

Photo Credits: canadastock/Shutterstock, cover; karp5/Shutterstock, 1; Pixfiction/Shutterstock, 3; Fedor Selivanov/Shutterstock, 4; bluejayphoto/iStock, 5; Bob Krist/Getty, 6-7; leoks/Shutterstock, 8-9; AB Visual Arts/Shutterstock, 10(background); Everett Historical/Shutterstock, 10(foreground); GLand Studio/Shutterstock, 10(frame); Everett Historical/Alamy, 11; Agencja Fotograficzna Caro/Alamy, 12-13; MagMac83/Shutterstock,14-15; Ikonoklast Fotografie/Shutterstock, 16; Michael Gottschalk/Getty, 17; kabVisio/iStock, 18-19; wojciech_gajda/iStock, 20-21, RomanR/Shutterstock, 23.

Printed in the United States of America at Corporate Graphics in North Mankato, Minnesota.

TABLE OF CONTENTS

CHAPTER 1

WELCOME TO GERMANY!

Willkommen! That is how you say "welcome" in Germany. Here you can walk historic streets. Discover beautiful castles. Or travel through a spooky forest.

Alps · · · · ▶

Germany is in Central Europe. Winters are cold and wet. Summers are warm. The Alps line the southern border. Snow covers this mountain range.

cuckoo
clock

Cuckoo clocks have been made here for 250 years! Where? The Black Forest **region**. It is in the south. The forest is thick. In some places, the sun cannot reach the forest floor.

WHAT DO YOU THINK?

The Brothers Grimm were from Germany. They collected fairy tales. The Black Forest may have inspired these stories. Like what? *Hansel and Gretel*. *Little Red Riding Hood*. What tales can you think of that take place in a forest?

The Rhine River is here. Barges use it to carry **cargo**. **Canals** link the Rhine to other rivers. Goods are traded with France. Belgium. The Netherlands. Like what? Grain. Minerals. Coal and oil products.

Rhine River

barge

CHAPTER 2

A LONG HISTORY

Germany was once ruled by a **monarchy**. The last king was Wilhelm II. He was forced to leave after World War I (1914–1918).

King Wilhelm II

Adolf Hitler came to power after the war. He told people he would make the country strong again. He led the people into a terrible war. It caused great destruction. More than 50 million people died in World War II (1939–1945). Germany lost.

The Soviet Union kept **military** in eastern Germany. A **communist** system of government was there. Three other countries had military in the west. What were they? The United States. England. France. The government was **democratic**. People had a better lifestyle there.

East Germans built the Berlin Wall. Why? To keep people from moving east to west. In 1989, the wall was torn down. People were free to go anywhere.

Berlin Wall

TAKE A LOOK!

Germany has had a long history of political events.

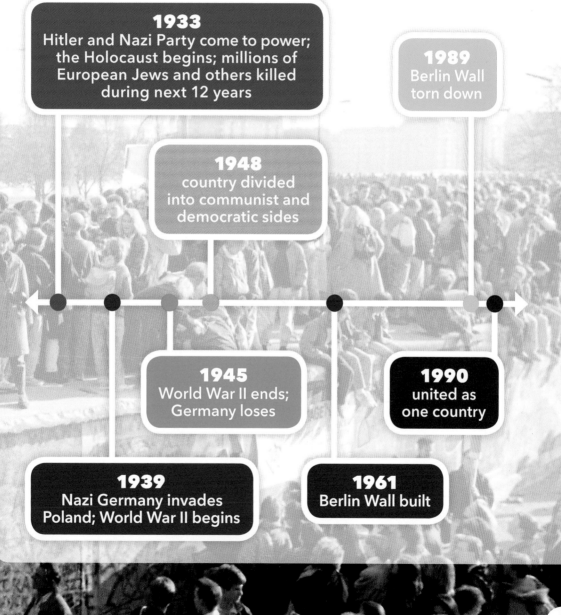

1933
Hitler and Nazi Party come to power; the Holocaust begins; millions of European Jews and others killed during next 12 years

1989
Berlin Wall torn down

1948
country divided into communist and democratic sides

1945
World War II ends; Germany loses

1990
united as one country

1939
Nazi Germany invades Poland; World War II begins

1961
Berlin Wall built

Today, Germans vote for lawmakers. They meet in the parliament building. It is in Berlin. This is the **capital**. The lawmakers elect a chancellor to lead the country.

DID YOU KNOW?

Three words are on the parliament building. What do they mean in English? "The German People."

DEM DEUTSCHEN VOLKE

CHAPTER 3

GERMANY'S PEOPLE

High school prepares students here for a **trade** or job. Many also go on to college. Some people have **service jobs**. They work in places like banks or restaurants.

Factory workers make cars and machinery. Farmers raise **livestock**. They grow grain and vegetables.

wurst · · · · ▶

The day begins with cereal, fruit, and toast. Lunch is the main meal. Schnitzel is fried meat. It is served with potatoes or noodles. Another favorite is wurst. It is like a hot dog.

People enjoy baked goods in the afternoon. Later, dinner is simple. Sandwiches and salads are common.

DID YOU KNOW?

Towns across the country enjoy Oktoberfest. It is held in fall. People dance and sing songs. They eat sausages. Chicken. And giant pretzels!

Germans cheer on favorite soccer teams. Tennis is popular, too. Some like to hike and ski in the Alps. Rivers and lakes offer fishing and swimming.

This is a beautiful country. Would you like to visit?

WHAT DO YOU THINK?

There are clubs for almost every sport and hobby in Germany. What are the benefits of belonging to a club? What club would you like to join?

QUICK FACTS & TOOLS

AT A GLANCE

North Sea

Baltic Sea

NETHERLANDS

Berlin ★

POLAND

GERMANY

BELGIUM

Rhine River

CZECH REPUBLIC

Alps

LUXEMBOURG

Black Forest

FRANCE

AUSTRIA

SWITZERLAND

N
W —|— E
S

GERMANY

Location: Central Europe

Size: 137,847 square miles (357,022 square kilometers)

Population: 80,594,017 (July 2017 estimate)

Capital: Berlin

Type of Government: federal parliamentary republic

Language: German

Exports: cars, machinery, chemicals, electronics

Currency: euro

canals: Water-filled channels dug across land so that boats can travel between two bodies of water.

capital: A city where government leaders meet.

cargo: Freight that is carried by a ship, plane, train, truck, or other vehicle.

communist: A type of government in which all land, property, businesses, and resources belong to the government.

democratic: A form of government in which the people choose their leaders in elections.

livestock: Animals that are kept or raised on a farm or ranch.

military: The armed forces of a country.

monarchy: A government in which the head of state is a king or queen.

region: A general area or a specific district or territory.

service jobs: Jobs and work that provide services for others, such as hotel, restaurant, and retail positions.

trade: A particular job, especially one that requires working with one's hands or machines.

Germany's currency

INDEX

TO LEARN MORE

Learning more is as easy as 1, 2, 3.

1) Go to www.factsurfer.com

2) Enter "Germany" into the search box.

3) Click the "Surf" button to see a list of websites.

With factsurfer, finding more information is just a click away.